101 Ways to Tell Your Child "I Love You"

VICKI LANSKY

Illustrations by Kaye Pomaranc White

CB

CONTEMPORARY
BOOKS

CHICAGO · NEW YORK

Library of Congress Cataloging-in-Publication Data

Lansky, Vicki.
  101 ways to tell your child "I love you."

  1. Parenting—Miscellanea.   2. Love, Maternal.
3. Love, Paternal.   I. Title.   II. Title: One hundred
one ways to tell your child "I love you."   III. Title:
One hundred and one ways to tell your child "I love
you."
HQ755.8.L354   1988   649'.1   88-20345
ISBN 0-8092-5427-2

Published by Contemporary Books, Inc.
180 North Michigan Avenue, Chicago, Illinois 60601
Manufactured in the United States of America
International Standard Book Number: 0-8092-4527-2

Published simultaneously in Canada by Beaverbooks, Ltd.
195 Allstate Parkway, Valleywood Business Park
Markham, Ontario L3R 4T8 Canada

To Doug and Dana,
the two favorite recipients of my
"I Love You's"

Introduction

Although it's an obvious thought, I was surprised to learn from an incident with my daughter that using the words *I love you* to say "I love you" isn't always enough. She had been a bit low for a day or two, and while the "I love you's" and hugs were there for her, they didn't seem to lift the cloud that hung over her. After one particularly pleasant day, I told her when I tucked her in at night how much I had *enjoyed* her that day. It was like flipping a light switch inside her. For many days afterward she would ask me, "Are you enjoying me?" Fortunately, I could usually answer YES!

There are many ways to show your children you love them. Love is shown in affection, in laughter, in private times together, in hugs and kisses, and in 101 other ways, such as those you'll find in this book. You may not use all of these wonderful ideas, for they will not all be comfortable for you or appropriate for your child's age. But I do think you'll find in this book many new and special ways to tell your child, "I love you." Have a terrific time trying those you like!

Vicki Lansky

Have a secret I LOVE YOU signal, maybe three squeezes of a hand, a V-sign with your fingers, or touching your nose and then your child's nose.

♡

Create fancy-named kisses to trade with your child, such as a "double chocolate chip," a "whipped cream mocha," or maybe an "orange meringue" kiss. Especially luscious at bedtime!

Make up a simple love song with your own words to an old tune, such as this one to the tune of "Frère Jacques":

"I love Susan, I love Susan.
She's a dear, she's a dear.
What a lovely daughter,
What a lovely daughter!
Glad she's here, glad she's here!"

Spontaneous gestures let your child know the fun side of love. Dad, stop in the middle of shaving to give a surprise shaving-cream kiss to your watching child, or stop in the middle of a bedtime story to give a big I LOVE YOU hug and kiss—just because you couldn't resist doing it!

♥

Learn to say "I love you" in sign language.

♡

Make up a photo album of your child for him or her to keep (kids love to look back on the "old days") or a scrapbook of first drawings or other precious memorabilia. Or help your child produce a ME book, complete with old and new photos, and lists of hobbies, interests, friends, toys, and pets.

♡

Share a special verse to let your child understand just how wonderful he or she is to you:

Leave a small surprise gift, such as stickers or a new marker, in an odd or unexpected place—in a pocket, a lunch box, or even in the

refrigerator. When asked "What for?" answer, "Because I love you, and I wanted to do something special for you."

♡

Lie outside on a blanket with your child on a fine summer night and watch for shooting stars.

Look steadily into your child's eyes, smile, but don't say a word for a few moments.

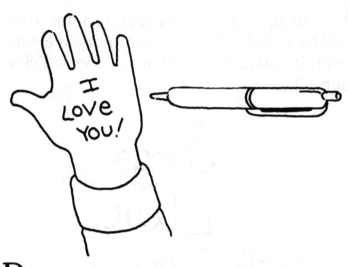

Draw a heart and the words I LOVE YOU on the back of your child's hand with a ballpoint pen. It's both naughty and nice!

Come up with a new anagram for your child's initials. For instance, Adrienne Gail Smith's initials might stand for **A**lways **G**iving **S**unshine.

<u>S</u>ings
<u>A</u>bout
<u>L</u>ove

Create an annual day for your child (Doug's Day, for example) on which your child has special privileges, such as answering the phone, riding in the front seat of the car, or pushing the elevator button. This makes a nice half-birthday celebration.

♡

Plant a kiss on your child's palm and roll the fingers tightly to "hold" it safely for later use, whenever it's needed.

Buy or make
personalized gifts;
anything with your
child's name on it
is special,

from personalized
barrettes and special-ordered pencils
to ironed-on letters on jeans or book bags.

♡

Leave surprise love messages in unexpected places—on the bathroom mirror, the front door . . . even on cereal boxes! Post-It™ notes work well here.

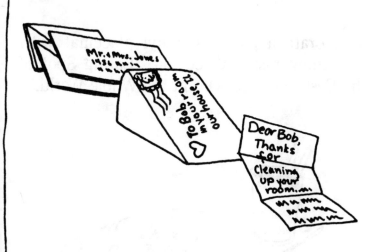

Mail a letter or card to your child, even if you haven't gone away. Getting mail is a special event for all children, especially at holiday times or when they are sick.

Decorate a paper or vinyl placemat with something personalized like "Eating Spot of the Best Four-Year-Old in the Whole World."

Rent or borrow a movie camera to make a video where your child is the star. Singing, dancing, and playing sports all make good center-stage performances.

♥

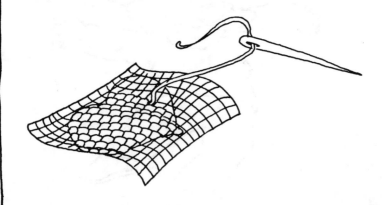

If you enjoy a craft such as needlecraft or woodworking, make your child a special present, such as a heart or his or her initials.

♡

Make a "monogram garden," indoors or out. In the yard, plant blossoming annuals of the same color in the shape of your child's name or

initials. Or indoors, you can sprout seeds on a large flat sponge floating on a shallow dish of water.

♡

Create bedtime stories in which your child is the hero or heroine in an adventure story. Or if you're reading aloud from a favorite book, change the name of the main character to that of your child.

♡

Let your child hear you praise him or her to others. Kids love to hear good things about themselves, especially when they "accidentally" overhear you.

Hang one or more red paper hearts by a
string or ribbon in your child's doorway,
for him or her to walk through as a
good-morning surprise or
when getting up
from a nap.

Say to your child, "I'm so glad God gave *you* to me!"

♡

Along with a good-night kiss, tell your child you appreciate all the good things he or she did that day, such as picking up toys or making the bed.

♡

Write a loving message on an inflated balloon for your child to find in an unexpected place, perhaps in the pantry, or even under the bedcovers. Filling a whole closet with balloons is even *more* memorable!

Create a "Welcome Home" or "I Love You" banner on computer paper or a roll of shelf paper as a surprise after the first day of school (or any other day!).

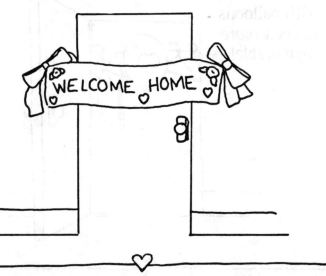

Serve your child's dinner on a special plate—
perhaps a china dish from your best set or a
favorite one that you keep on display—to cele-
brate a triumph or act as a reminder on a bad
day that he or she is still very important to
you.

♥

Have a discussion about the color of love. Ask your child what color love is, and why.

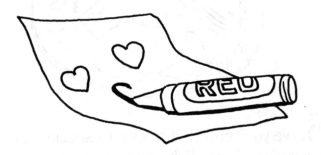

Later you can use that color in gift-giving or gift-wrapping so your child will know that it is given with *extra* love.

Leave praising announcements such as "I Love Leslie's Smile" on your refrigerator, kitchen chalkboard, or other family message center, for all to see. You can also post report cards and other special awards.

♡

Design homemade cards (using stencils, stickers, or markers) to show that special feeling of love and caring. It's a good idea to stock up on such items as heart stickers and note pads in January and February (Valentine's Day) to pass on your love all through the year.

♡

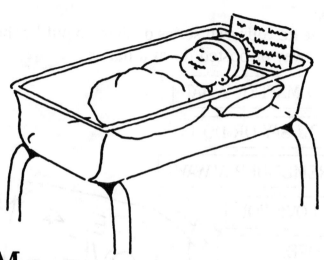

Make an outing to the hospital where your child was born, and tell about his or her birth-day. Stop at the nursery during visiting hours to see the new babies.

♡

Create your own series of signs to put by the driveway or posted down a hallway.

NO MATTER WHAT

YOU SAY OR DO

REMEMBER ALWAYS

I LOVE YOU

LOVE,
   MOM/DAD

"I like the way you . . ." is a loving message for a child to hear, appropriate for anything from brushing hair or licking an ice cream cone.

♡

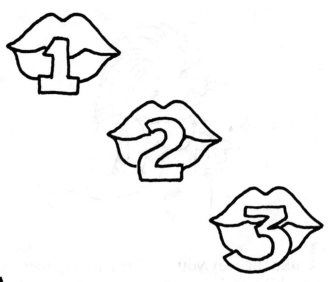

Ask your child to pick a number from 1 to 10. Then deliver that many kisses!

Pick a nickname for your child that will enhance his or her self-image. "Sara Sharer," for example, or "Josh the Joyful," or "Doug the Daring."

Let your child crawl into bed with you in the morning for a snuggle if last night's bedtime hug was missed . . . or even if it wasn't!

♡

Let your children know that they are—*and will be*—loveable at every age. Tell a 5-year-old, "I'm going to love you when you are 6 years old . . . when you are 16 years old . . .

when you are 26 years old . . . and even when you are 60 years old." Or simply say, ". . . and when you're all grown-up!"

♡

Lay out a secret treasure hunt for your child with a map or a series of clues that will lead from one room to the next. The treasure is an I LOVE YOU message and a surprise such as a book, toy, or an IOU for a trip to the zoo.

♥

Say "I love you" in pig Latin:

"I-ya ov-lay ou-yay!"

A delightful verbal game that you can make one of your family traditions is the following exchange:

Parent: "Have I told you how much I love you today?"

Child: "No!"

Parent: "I love you, I love you, I love you." (smooch, smooch, smooch)

With lipstick, write a love message or draw a heart on the bathroom mirror for your children to see when they brush their teeth in the morning.

P lay "I love you more than . . . ." You can begin with, "I love you more than all the leaves on the trees," and then move on to ". . . all the ice cream in the world . . . stars in the sky," and so on. Then let your child come up with some of his or her own.

There are two sides of love.

One is giving, the other
receiving. Children
sometimes show us
their love when
we're busy or angry,
but we need to *let* them
show it when they
want to.

After all,
that's how *we* do it.

♡

Children with brothers and sisters don't always understand that there is enough of their parents' love to go around in a family. Using candles, you can show how your love can be

shared without it being diminished. Light one candle to represent Mom, and from that one light another for Dad. Then one for each child. Each flame is as bright as the others.

♡

Let a hand puppet or stuffed animal talk for you, telling your child how much you love him or her, and nuzzling up to dispense kisses.

D‍o you have an "I Love You Up To Here" chart? It's a great way to mark your child's height periodically, on a door frame or a large piece of poster board.

Wake your child up with a kiss. What nicer or more loving way is there to start a day?

Write "I love (your child's name)" with chalk on a sidewalk, driveway, or porch as a public display of affection.

Let your children know how special it is to be their parent by saying, "I love being your mom," "I love being your dad," or "I love you for making my life wonderful."

♡

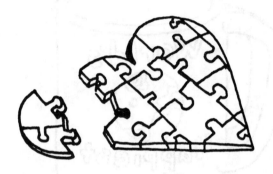

Make a heart-shaped I LOVE YOU puzzle.
On a piece of cardboard, write your message
(such as "I love you 2 pieces"), then cut it up
so your child can put it back together.

♡

Take your child on a secret destination car ride, maybe even blindfolding him or her until you are there. "There" can be an ice cream parlor, a favorite scenic spot, or just a play- ground or park.

Write I LOVE YOU on a ball and play catch with it. With every toss, your child will be "catching" a bit of love from you.

♡

Create a family hug as one of your traditions, where everyone huddles together and shares hugs and kisses.

See how many words you and your child can make from the letters, I L-O-V-E Y-O-U.

Make an I LOVE YOU heart-shaped cake.

Step #1

Step #2

Step #3

Make an oral "love list" of your child's face: "I love your nose . . . your ears . . . your eyes"—and give a kiss for each.

Go for a walk in the moonlight, or in a new winter snow, or even in a warm summer rain, for a special memorable event.

Put your ear to your child's belly button, saying that you are listening to a little voice in there. After a moment, announce, "I hear a request for a hug." Then comply!

Take turns in this little rhyming game:

I Love You..........Yes, I do!
I Love You..........Wouldn't you?
I Love You..........I'd wear your shoe.
I Love You..........Kiss me, too.

See how many you and your child can make up!

Look up the word LOVE in the dictionary together. Then remind your child that that's how you feel about him or her.

Love (lŭv) *n.* 1. An intense feeling....

♡

Create a LOVE collage of your child's name, initials, and personal interests. Cut out words, letters, and pictures from magazines or newspapers to spell out your message, and glue them all on a piece of posterboard.

♡

If you leave the house before your kids get up in the morning, leave a love note under each glass of breakfast juice you've poured for them.

♥LOVE LICENSE♥

NAME _____ _____
                        (EYES)
is licensed to love and be loved!

ADDRESS _____ _____
                                 (AGE)

CITY/STATE _____

X _____
              SIGNATURE
VALID FOREVER AND EVER AND EVER!

Make up a "Love License" on an index card. First design one for your child, and then help him or her make them for the rest of the family.

Give your children framed family pictures for their bedrooms. Be sure to sign them, with love.

♥

After disciplining your child, an important loving message is, "I don't always like your *behavior*, but I always love *you*."

Give "Eskimo" kisses by rubbing noses! Or an "angel's kiss" by kissing a child's shut eyelids!

♡

Going out for the evening? Try some pillow talk. Write a love note and leave it on your child's pillow for him or her or the sitter to

read at bedtime. If the child is old enough, encourage a response on your pillow to welcome you home. (Don't forget to use the universal code for hugs and kisses . . . ooxxoo!)

Serve Jiggle Jell-O™ Hearts, which are made by using heart-shaped cookie cutters on extra-firm gelatin:

2 envelopes unflavored gelatin
2½ cups water
1 large package (6 ounces) red Jell-O™

Soften the unflavored gelatin in 1 cup of cool water. In a saucepan, bring 1 cup of water to a boil and add the Jell-O. Remove from heat. Stir until dissolved. Add the softened gelatin, stir, and add the last ½ cup of water. Pour into a lightly greased 8-inch square pan and refrigerate until firm. Cut with cookie cutters.

♥

When was the last time you gave a *bear hug*? No matter what the child's age, a caring, crushing hug is memorable. Try to be the last one to let go—you'll leave behind a wonderful feeling.

When you travel, try to bring home a small gift: a hotel note pad and pen or an accordian picture postcard set from the city you've visited. It's a great way to say, "I really thought of you when I was gone."

♡

Here's a "knock, knock" joke that delights!

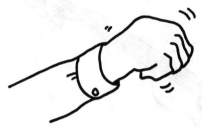

Knock, Knock
Who's there?
Olive
Olive who?
Olive you!

♡

Serenade your child with cute love songs like, "I Love You a Bushel and a Peck" or "You Are My Sunshine."

Hang mistletoe even when the holidays are over to assure a constant supply of hugs and kisses.

Bring home a flower
for your child,
or even a
whole bouquet!

Make heart-shaped sandwiches by cutting sliced bread with a cookie cutter. For a pretty, open-faced heart-shaped sandwich, mix softened cream cheese with a bit of red food coloring and a drop or so of milk.

♡

Make up I LOVE YOU coupons to give as a gift . . . just because "I love you." These can be for: staying up an hour late, picking a special TV show, making cookies together, playing a favorite board or card game, or buying a pack of gum at the grocery store.

Out of cardboard,
make large coins and print
on them,
    GOOD FOR A HUG.
To be redeemed as needed!

Draw the letters I L-O-V-E Y-O-U on your child's back with your finger during a bedtime backrub.

Send a secret I LOVE YOU message that must be turned toward a mirror to be read, or decoded with a secret code.

♡

Decorate a little bag of loving surprises and put it near your child's bed to be found in the morning. You might include a little chalkboard, a small book, some balloons, or maybe even a piece of fruit.

♡

Make LOVE ME cracker snacks. On a round cracker, put a cheese spread, olive slices for

eyes, raisins for a smiley mouth, and a red-hot heart for a nose.

Let your children know that distance doesn't lessen love. When you travel, tell them you think of them when you're up in the plane flying through the clouds. Also, let them know that their relatives who live far away love them and think of them a lot.

♡

In how many languages can you say "I love you"?

I Love You	Language	Sounds Like
je t'aime	French	*je tem*
te amo	Spanish	tay ahmo
ich liebe dich	German	ick leebe dick
lo tiamo	Italian	yo teeahmo

Make special hamburgers by "decorating" them with hearts, using ketchup from a squeeze bottle.

♡

Label a jar "Hugs and Kisses," and fill it with slips of paper that say "I need a hug," "I need a kiss," and "I need both a hug and a kiss." Then let your child select one every day, perhaps at bedtime.

♡

Teach your child how to make pretty paper hearts, using folded colored paper or heart-shaped cookie cutters to trace.

Make a pennant for your child's wall from a
triangular piece of paper or felt, and decorate it

with his or her initials, the words *I Love You*,
and plenty of hearts.

A surprise breakfast in bed will make the day really special.

Fill a large jar with nuts, add a ribbon to make it festive, and attach a note that says "I'm nuts about you "

Let your child select
one night's dinner
menu—especially
the dessert!

How many ways are there to say "You're great!"?

There's nothing like cuddling up with kids and a good book to show them how much you love them, as well as how much fun it is to read.

M ake an alphabet cereal message: spell out

I LOVE YOU

on top of toast or just on the plate.

Write a secret message-in-pictures.

Or disguise a message with this code that children love to use: A=1; B=2; C=3; etc.

For a shortcut:

9/12-15-22-5/25-15-21

I L O V E Y O U

Come up behind your child, put your hands over his or her eyes, and say:

"Somebody loves you
Who could it be?

Now you see,
The one who loves you is me!"

Pluck daisy petals for "I love you, I love you not."

(Be sure to end up with "I love you"!)

♡

Just once, place a freshly lipsticked smooch on your child's cheek, forehead, or hand to "show" your love.

♡

Use the letters in your child's name to create a personal note or colorful poster:

D is for Delightful
A is for Affectionate
N is for Nearly perfect
A is for Animated

Make sure you have a will naming a suggested guardian and executor. It is the most loving and thoughtful thing you can do for your child.

♡

What are your family's favorite "I Love You's"?
Send yours to: Vicki Lansky
                 c/o Practical Parenting
                 Department L
                 Deephaven, MN 55391

For a free catalog of Vicki Lansky's other books, just drop a note to the above address or call 1-800-255-3379.